Blueberry Muffins

By Heather Hammonds
Illustrations by Pat Reynolds
Photographs by Lyz Turner-Clark

Contents

Muffins for Grandma

Toby came into the kitchen.
It was Grandma's birthday
and Mum was making
a chicken salad for lunch.

Can I make something special
for Grandma?

2

Yes, but she will be here
in half an hour.
There won't be much time
to make something big.

Toby looked in Mum's cook book.

Grandma likes chocolate cake. I could make her a chocolate cake and put cherries on the top.

Toby turned to another page in the cook book.

I could make this sponge.
The recipe says it's as light as a feather.

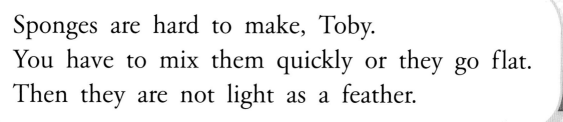

Sponges are hard to make, Toby.
You have to mix them quickly or they go flat.
Then they are not light as a feather.

Then, Toby remembered something.

I know, Mum!
I could make some blueberry muffins
for Grandma.
I'm good at making muffins.

You are right. I'll help you.
Let's get started now.
We have just enough time
to get them cooked
before Grandma arrives.

An Email to Dad

To: Chef_TomBarnes@navy_ships.com

Dear Dad,
Today it was Grandma's birthday.
She had lunch at our house.

Mum made chicken salad for lunch.
I wanted to make something
very special for Grandma.

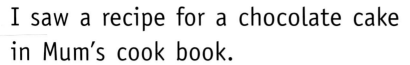

I saw a recipe for a chocolate cake
in Mum's cook book.
The cake had cherries on the top,
but Mum said that chocolate cakes
take too long to cook.
We didn't have any cherries either,
because I had eaten them
for breakfast.

Then, I saw a recipe for a sponge,
but that was not a good idea.
Mum said that sponges are hard to make
because you have to mix them quickly
or they go flat.

Then, I remembered that I can cook really good blueberry muffins.
Mum helped me and they were ready just before Grandma arrived.

Then, I remembered that I can cook
really good blueberry muffins.
Mum helped me and they were ready
just before Grandma arrived.

Grandma loved the muffins.
She told me that they were
the best muffins
she had ever tasted.

Love from,
Toby